Paper Quilling Patterns for Beginners

DEDICATION

Contents

How to Make Paper Quilling Flowers 2

Paper Quilling Tips for Beginners 10

DIY Paper Quilling Fall Tree Craft 19

Paper Quilled Snowflake Ornaments 27

How to Make a Paper Quilled Monogram 33

How to Make Paper Quilling Flowers

Paper quilling, also called paper filigree, is the art of rolling, scrolling, and shaping paper strips into delightful designs. Quilling is not new; it has been around since the 15th century but is just as well-liked today as it was hundreds of years ago. This hobby is very easy to learn, doesn't cost a lot of money, and produces beautiful works of art in a short period of time. No wonder it has been popular for hundreds of years!

Flowers are one of the most beloved designs in quilling, and this tutorial concentrates on making a simple daisy from strips of paper. Learn how to make the flower from two paper shapes, and you will soon be on your way to creating more beautiful paper filigree projects.

If you are a complete beginner, you probably already have the simple supplies in your house to get started. Of course, it makes the job easier if you purchase some basic quilling tools, including pre-cut strips of paper to make your flowers neatly curled. However, you can always cut your paper strips by hand.

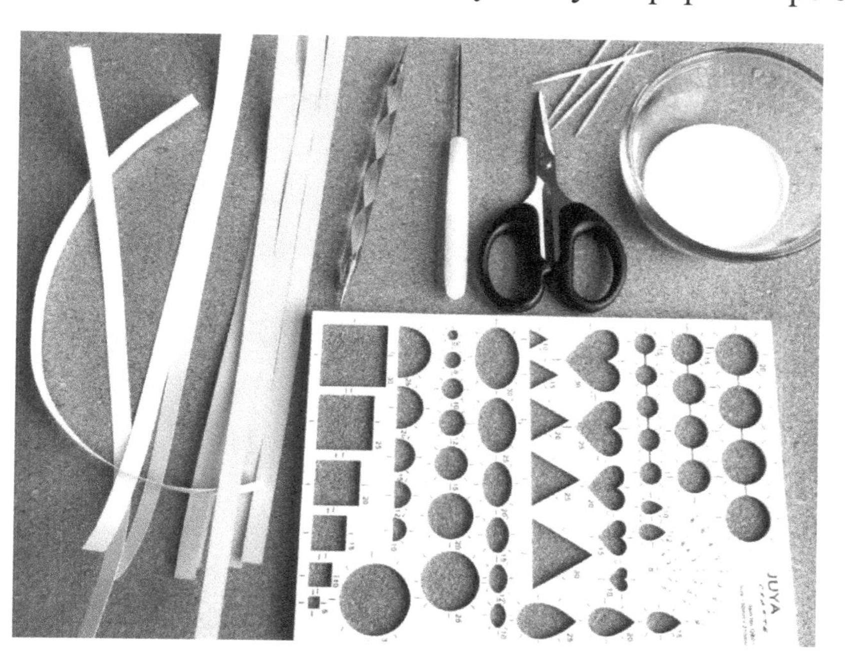

What You'll Need

Equipment / Tools

Quilling board

Slotted quilling tool

Needle quilling tool

Toothpicks, Scissors

Paper trimmer/cutter (if cutting paper strips by hand)

Craft glue

Straight pins Hot glue , Tweezers , Ruler (optional)

Materials

Paper for strips or pre-cut paper quilling strips approximately

Small flower pot (optional)

Floral foam (optional)

Thin wood dowels or wood skewers (optional)

Artificial Spanish moss (optional)

Instructions

Step1: Construct the Daisy Petals

- You will need to cut six white paper strips to make the daisy petals.
- Cut strips to measure 3/8 inches wide by 12 inches long. If you are using pre-cut quilling paper strips, you may need to cut them down.
- To make a paper petal, you first have to take a piece of paper and insert it into the slot of the slotted quilling tool.
- Hold the tool in your hand between your thumb and index finger and slowly turn the tool so the paper winds evenly around the tip.
- Pull the coil from the tool and place it into a circle on the quilling board, and allow the coil to unwind until it is the size of the circle.

- Remove the paper coil and glue the end of the strip and let it dry. You may then squeeze the paper coil into different shapes.

Note: Using a Template Board

Our board is sized in millimeters, and we used the 25-millimeter circle template, which is a little under 1 inch. If your template board has circles sized in inches, use the 1-inch circle template for your petals.

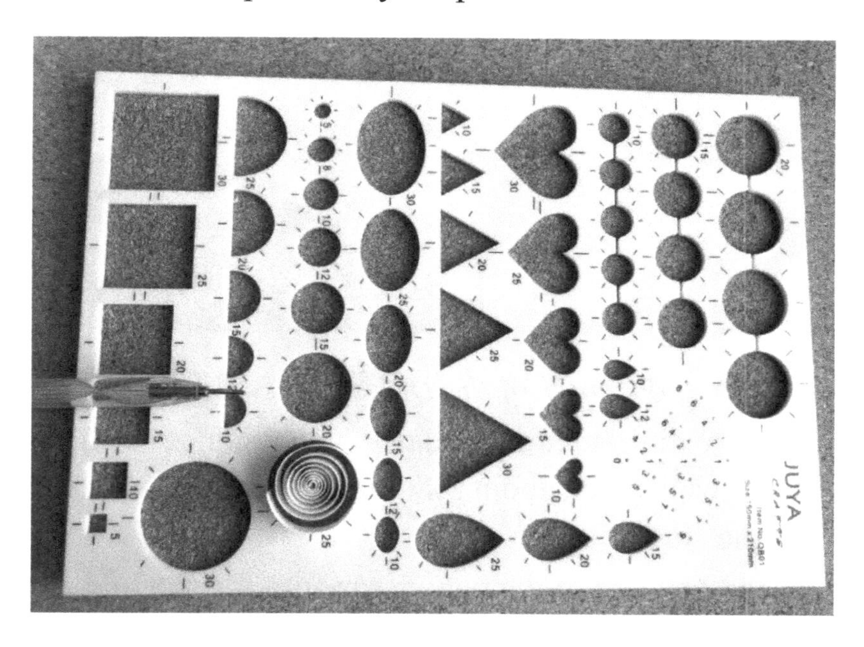

Step2: Squeeze the Paper Coil Into a Teardrop Shape

- To form a paper coil into a teardrop shape, you must first pull the inside of the coil gently downwards and hold while pinching one side of the circle to form a point. Your paper circle will now be in a teardrop shape.

- Make six paper teardrop shapes to form the petals of your quilled daisy.

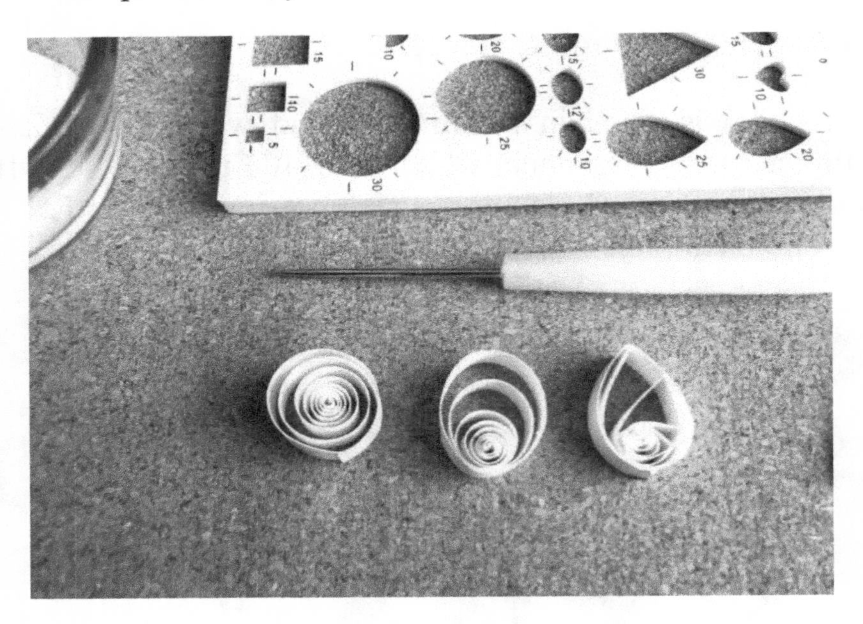

Step 3. Make the Center of the Daisy

- To make the center of the daisy, you will need two colored paper strips (each about 3/8 inch wide and 12 inches long) and the slotted tool.
- Thread one end of the paper strip into the slot and turn the tool making sure to maintain tension.
- After you form the center coil place some glue on the end of the paper strip and let it dry. Do not remove the coil from the tool.
- Place a bit of glue onto the rolled coil and place another paper strip aligned with the end of the first paper strip.
- Roll the second paper strip onto the coil, maintaining tension.

- Add some glue to the end of the second paper strip.
- Let the glue dry.
- Remove the tight coil from the slotted tool.

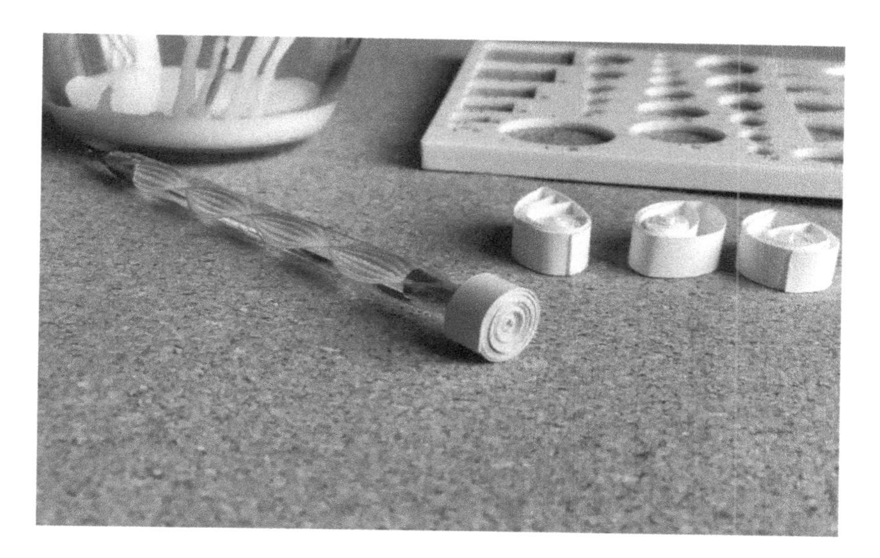

Step 4: Glue Together Your Quilled Shapes

- Arrange the six teardrop petals around the paper coil to form the flower shape.
- Glue the teardrops to the paper coil and to the sides of each teardrop shape.
- Let the glue completely dry.
- After the flower dries you will be able to pick it up and it should hold its shape.

  Note: Gluing Quills in Place
- There are many tips on how to handle delicate quilled parts. Here are two tips that help when gluing them together.

- Tweezers makes it easier to arrange the small

place and while gluing them together.

- Using straight pins helps to keep the quilled rolls in place until the glue dries.

Step 5. Plant Your Flowers

Quilled flowers can be used in card projects, scrapbooking, wall hangings, and as welcoming signs of springtime. Here's how we displayed our flowers in a flowerpot:

- Hot glue some thin wooden dowels or skewers onto the back of the flowers.
- Pl oral foam into a small flower pot.
- wers on wood "stems" into the floral foam.
- p of the pot opening with artificial Spanish t a delightful way to welcome spring or

quills into

Paper Quilling Tips for Beginners

Eight Tips to Help You Become a Paper Quilling Pro

Step 1: Use Pre-cut Paper Strips for Your First Projects

Use pre-cut paper quilling strips for your first projects. Your initial attempts will have better results if you use precise machine-cut papers. Once you are comfortable with basic paper quilling techniques, you can cut your paper strips and explore your creativity by experimenting with more advanced methods

Step 2. Start With Small Paper Quilling Projects

Start with smaller sized projects first. You can quickly become overwhelmed when trying to tackle a craft project that is too complicated or too large. Small projects can promote feelings of success and accomplishment and can be the building blocks the help you master your skills one step at a time. Once you have mastered the basics, you can attempt complicated projects with ease.

Step 3. Use the Right Paper Quilling Tools

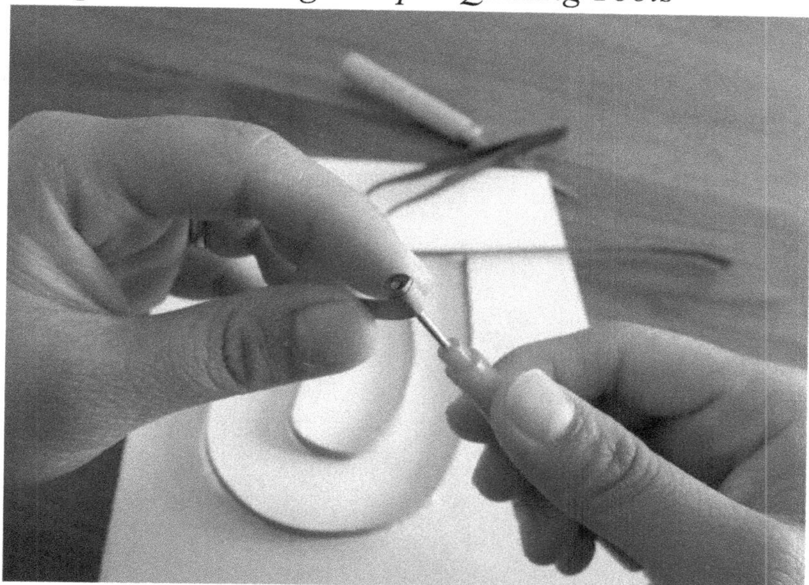

It's important to choose your quilling tools thoughtfully. You don't need to buy any expensive tools to create paper filigree art initially–a toothpick or bamboo skewer will roll paper strips adequately. If you are bitten by the paper quilling bug and wish to continue, you should purchase a slotted quilling tool and a needle tool.

You can place the strip of paper into the upper slot of the slotted tool, giving you more control when rolling the paper strips. A needle device is a sizeable tapered needle with a long wooden handle. It helps you keep a steady hand when rolling strips of paper into various shapes. Both tools are quite helpful when you are working on large, complicated paper quilling projects.

Step 4.Have a Light Touch When Using Glue with Paper Quilling

When gluing your rolled paper shapes, always remember to use glue sparingly. Too much glue can quickly ruin your project, which you may have worked on for hours. You can avoid the hassle of starting a project over with a little bit of caution. You can always add a bit more adhesive if necessary, but cannot remove excess glue. Remember the design rule "Less is More."

Step 5. Paper Quilling Patterns

Some beginners find using a premade quilling pattern quite helpful when first starting out. There are hundreds of paper quilling patterns available for purchase or free download on the internet. These printable patterns can guide beginners and help them build their skills.

All you have to do is place the printed pattern under a sheet of waxed paper and follow the suggestions. You will quickly have a quilling "masterpiece" that you will be proud to give as a gift or display in your home.

Step 6. Master the Basic Paper Quilling Shapes

Quilling Shapes

Coil or Circle Shapes	*Scroll and Spiral Shapes*
Tight Coil	*Loose Scroll*
Loose Coil	*S – Scroll*
Teardrop	*C – Scroll*
Marquis	*Heart Scroll*
Heart	*Spiral*

Learn the basic shapes before working on a paper quilling project. It can be quite helpful to make a master page of basic paper quilling shapes.

Glue different shapes to a piece of cardboard to use as a reference sheet when working on various projects. The guide serves as both a reference and an inspiration source.

Step 7. Paper Quilling Circle Sizing Board

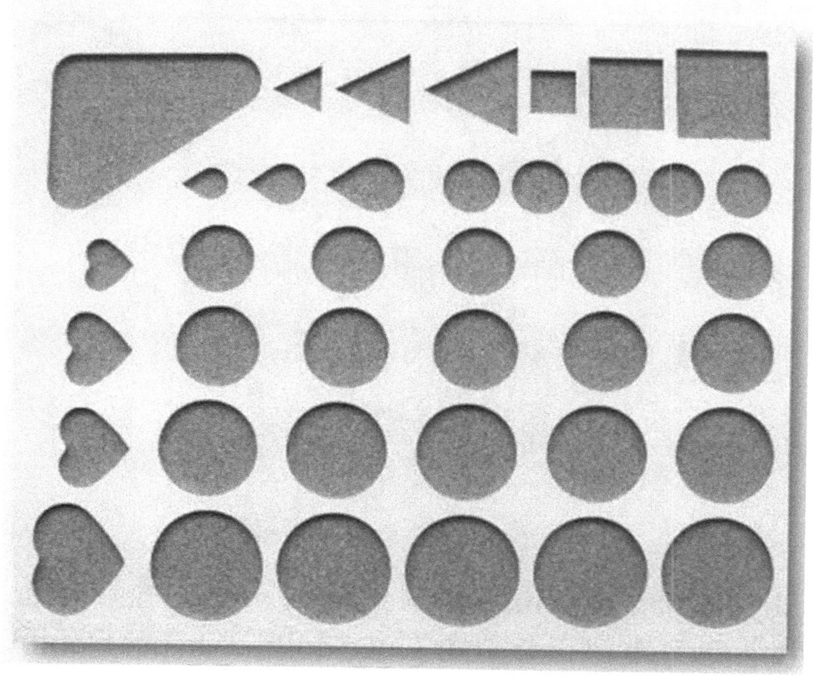

A circle sizing board is a tool you definitely will find useful. It is a sheet of plastic that has predrilled holes of various shapes and sizes. Use the holes to help you roll the paper quilling shapes.

The circle sizing board will help you will always have consistency in your paper quilling shapes. This board is a tool you won't want to be without and will use again and again.

Step 8. Acetate Sheet

Build your paper quilling rolled shape onto a sheet of acetate. It is strong enough to give your glued quilled shapes stability. After the glue has dried, you can pull your quilled piece up off the sheet without damage. Just wash the leftover adhesive from the acetate sheet and reuse for your next project.

Paper Quilling Closing Thoughts

These are just a few tips to help you get started on your paper quilling journey. Remember that it will take awhile to master the craft, so be patient with yourself and practice. You will find that if you keep at it, you will amaze yourself with your progress. You will soon be making pieces of quilling art that are beautiful and will be treasured by you and everyone you give a paper quilling project as a gift.

DIY Paper Quilling Fall Tree Craft

List of Supplies to make the Paper Quilling Fall Tree Craft

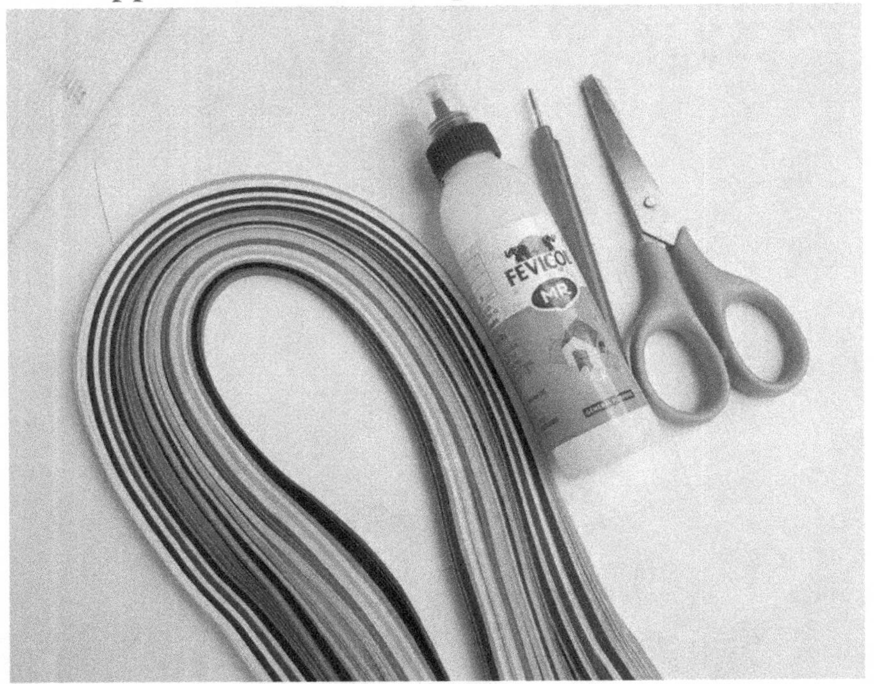

01. Quilling paper strips – 5mm – Red, Yellow, Orange, Brown
02. White cardstock 6 x 12 inches
03. Craft glue
04. Slotted quilling tool
05. ScissorsInstructions to make the Paper Quilling Fall Tree Craft

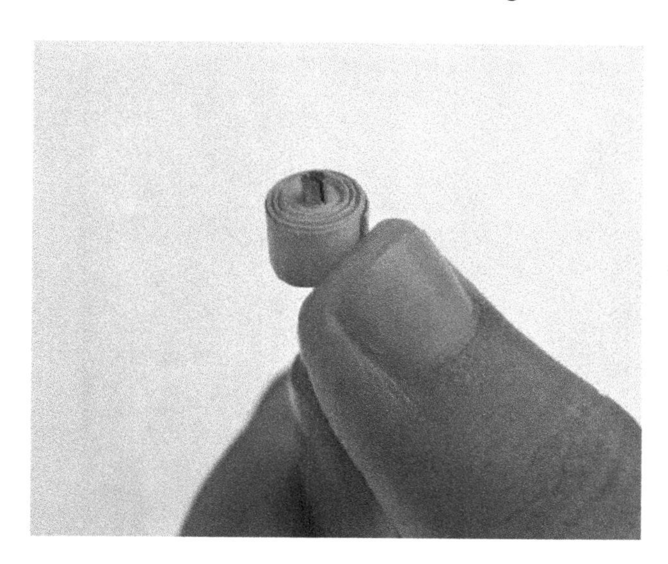

Select 3-4 fall colored quilling strips. Take a 10-inch long quilling strip and coil the entire strip with the help of the slotted quilling tool

Take out the coiled strip out of the slotted tool and allow the coil o loosen up a little. Glue the open end to secure the loose coil hape.

Press any one side of the loose coil prepared in the previous step to create a teardrop shape. We have created a teardrop shape.

Now press the opposite side of the coils' previously pressed side to create a basic eye shape. Glue the open end of the strip to secure the shape.

Similarly, create more basic eye shapes using fall colored quilling strips. These will be the leaves.

Take brown colored quilling strips and cut them into any customized size you want, mine were 5 inches long. Use the slotted tool to coil about 1 or 1.5 inches of the strip from any one end.

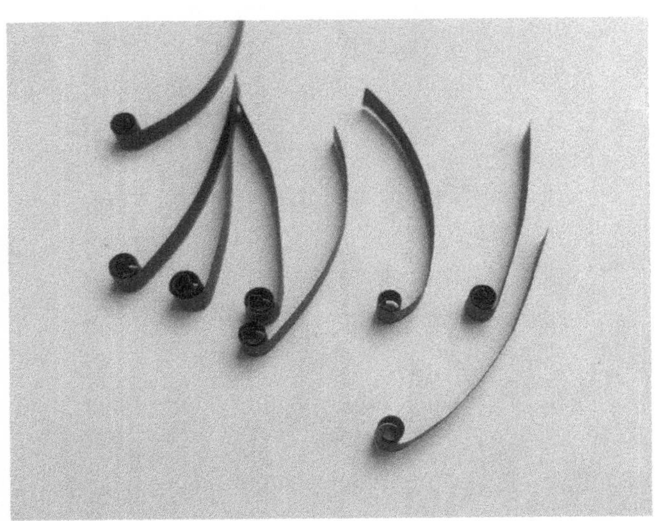

Similarly, prepare 6 to 8 more strips as prepared in the previous step.

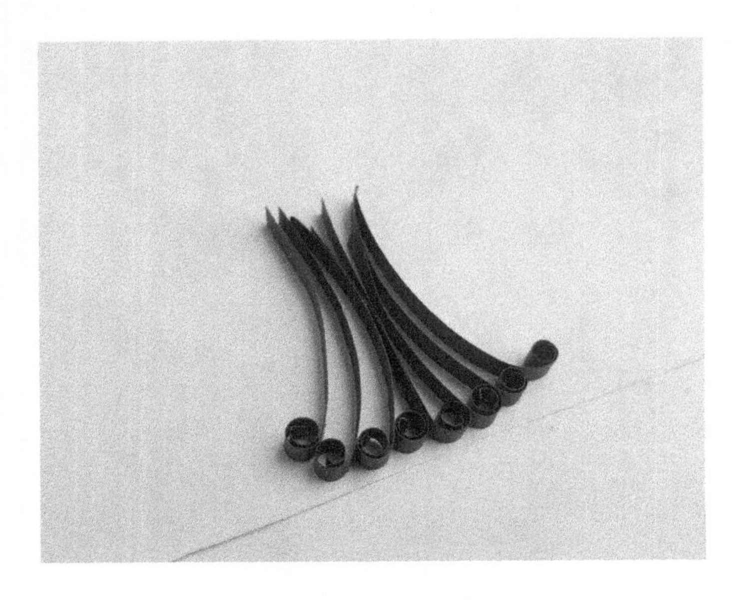

Fold a piece of white cardstock paper in half to form a card.. Glue the strips prepared in step 7 on the paper; basically creating the trunk of the tree.

Now take the basic eye shapes (leaves) and start to stick them above the trunk pattern.

While sticking the leaf shapes try to keep a nice pattern combination. I glued 3 to 4 basic eye shapes in groups.

All done? You can stop once you are satisfied with the tree pattern. Allow the glue to dry.

And done!

Paper Quilled Snowflake Ornaments

Material

Paper quilling strips 5mm wide and 54cm long – White , Blue

Quilling slotted tool or a toothpick with a slot cut at the back.

Glue

Scissors

Plastic sheet/ grease proof paper

Pencil

Geometric compass

White sheet of paper

Small ruler

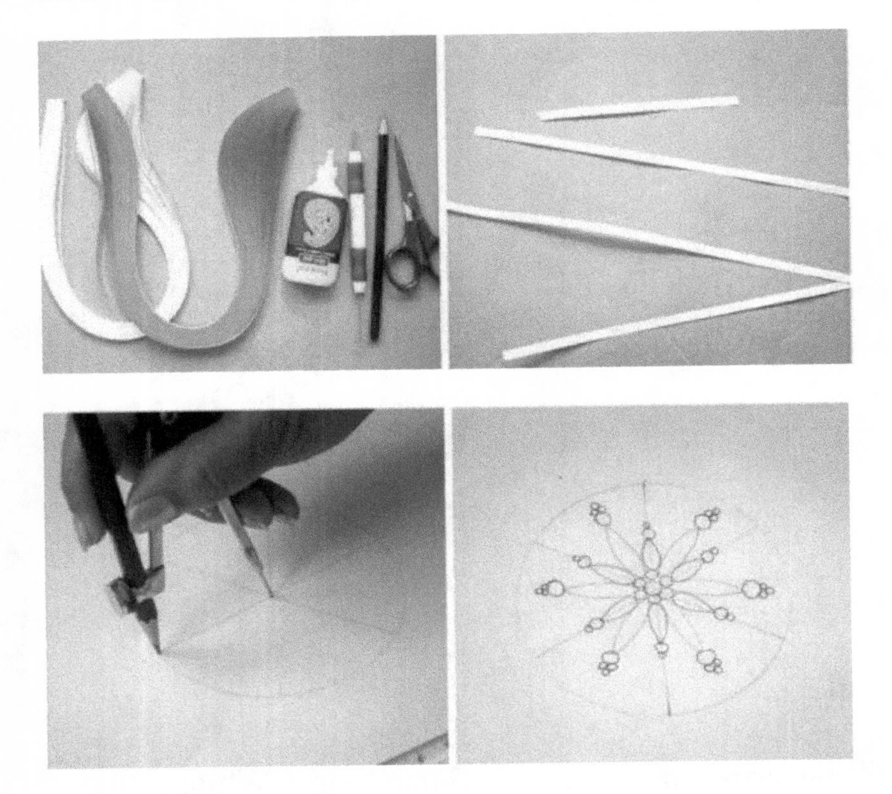

01. The first step is to identify the length of the strips for your quilled snowflakes. We have used the full length, the half & the quarter length.

02. Using a compass, draw a 5 cm circle on the white sheet. This will be the base of our design.
03. Next, divide the circle into 6 equal parts and draw your design. We used 3 basic quilling folds to make the snowflake – Tight Coil, Teardrop & Marquis.
04. For the first fold – Tight Coil, roll a strip around a slotted tool tightly. Glue the end firmly in place

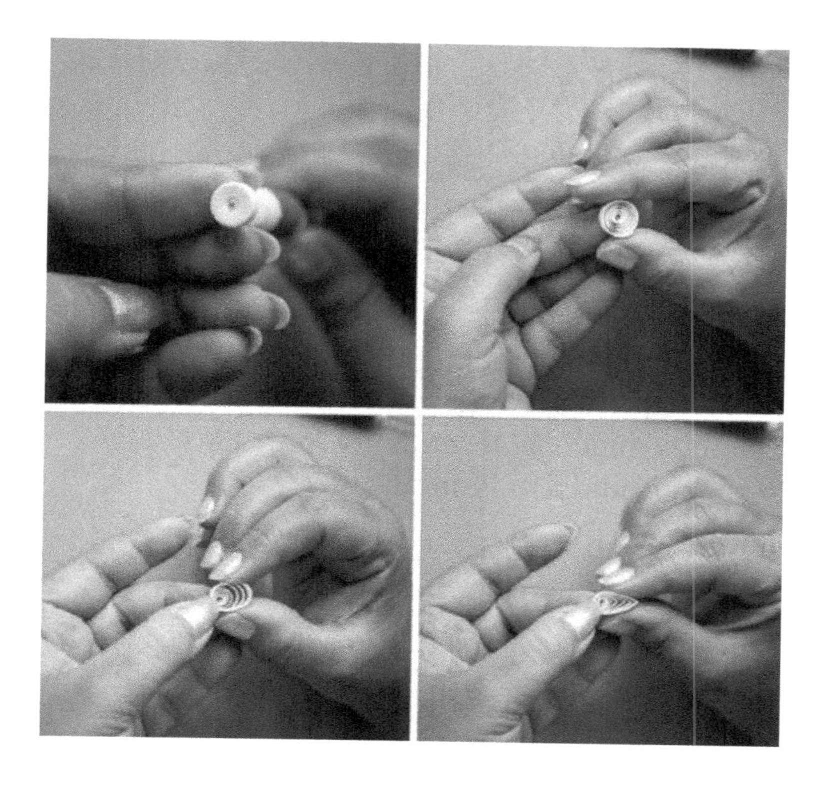

05. For the second fold – Teardrop, roll a strip around a slotted tool tightly. Gently take it out of the tool, let it expand between two fingers. Now with the other hand, slightly pinch one end to form a leaf or a teardrop like structure. Glue the end firmly in place

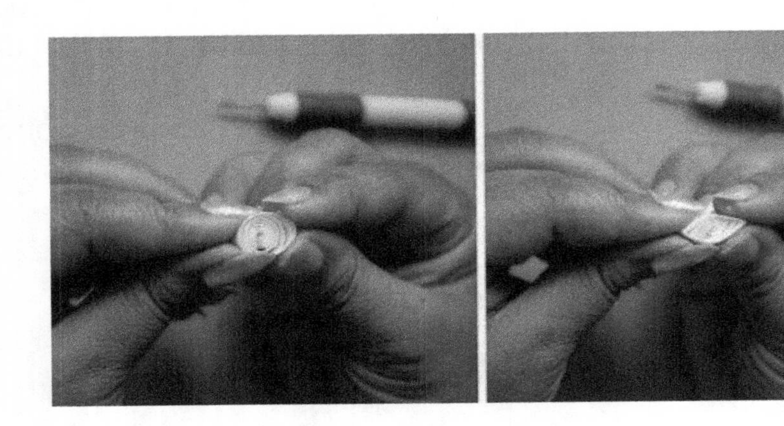

06. For the third fold – The marquis or the eye, roll a strip around a slotted tool tightly. Gently take it out of the tool, let it expand between two fingers. Now with both hands, slightly pinch both ends to form an eye like structure. Glue the end firmly in place

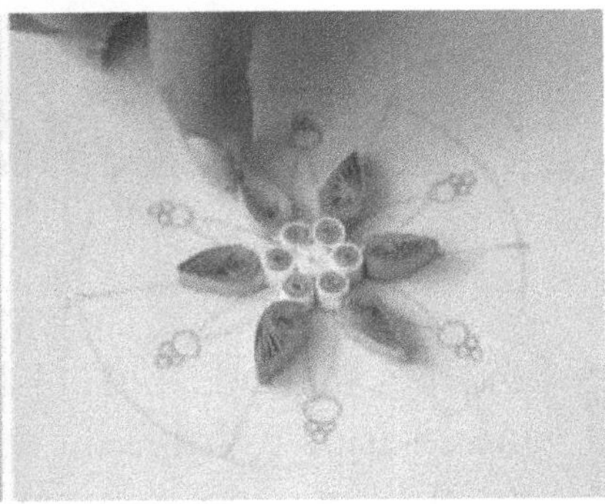

07. For the snowflake we need

- 6 full length marquis in white,
- 6 full length teardrops in blue,
- 6 full length tight coils in white,
- 1 half-length tight coil in white,
- 6 half-length tight coils in blue,
- 18 quarter-length tight coils in blue and
- 6 quarter-length marquis in white.

We wrapped a quarter-length strip around some of the pieces to make our design prettier.

08. We are ready to assemble. Place the drawing under an OHP sheet and start assembling each piece from the center out. First the white half tight coil. Stick the blue quarter coils around it. Then stick the teardrops using the drawing below as reference. The white marquis in between and finally the teardrops & mini marquis at the ends. You could make your own design really, there is no script here. We made three snowflakes all using the same folds.

09. Let it dry completely so that each fold is stuck firmly to the one next to it. You could coat it modge podge or spray a clear varnish over it, but that's not necessary.
10. String some bakers twine and you have a little snowflake adorning your Christmas tree.

How to Make a Paper Quilled Monogram

Working Time: 60 mins

Total Time: 4 hrs

Yield: 1 monogram

Skill Level: Beginner

letter R quilled monogram

What You'll Need

Equipment / Tools

Scissors

Craft paper trimmer

Tweezers

Tacky glue (such as Mod Podge)

1 Paper plate or old plastic container for glue

Small paintbrush for glueing

Materials

Card stock or pre-cut quilling strips in desired colors

1 sheet Thick card stock or board for the background

1 Shadowbox picture frame

Instructions

Step1 .Print Your Outline

Print your letter of choice, filled in with a light or dark background color of your choice, onto the card stock background.

Note: Alternative Letter Method

If you don't have access to a printer, use this alternative method for a letter:

- Trace a large letter from a source, such as a book or magazine, onto a sheet of paper using a pencil.
- Use a light touch with the pencil, you don't want to see the pencil lines in your final project. It will be hard to erase the lines after you build your frame.
- Or, you can fill in the letter with a preferred background color that will peek out from under quilled pieces.
- Use a ruler to make the straight lines.
- If desired, attach the paper with the tracing onto a piece of card stock for the added stability.

Step2. Cut the Strips

- Choose card stock in colors you plan to incorporate into your design.
- Use the paper cutter to cut paper strips from the card stock that measure one-quarter inch wide.

Note: Pre-Cut Card Stock Strips

Instead of cutting strips, buy packages of pre-cut quilling paper online or at the craft store.

Step 3. Shape the Strips

Once you decide what the design of the inside of your letter will be, it's time to make shapes.

- Take a paper strip and wind it around your toothpick or quilling tool into the shape desired, either rolled tightly (for a compact shape) or loosely, depending on your preference. Refer to the common quilling shapes below.
- Place a tiny bit of glue onto the end of the paper strip to hold the shape in place.

Note: Sketch It Out

Before curling your strips, look at other quilled monograms for inspiration and make a preliminary quick thumbnail sketch for the layout of your monogram.

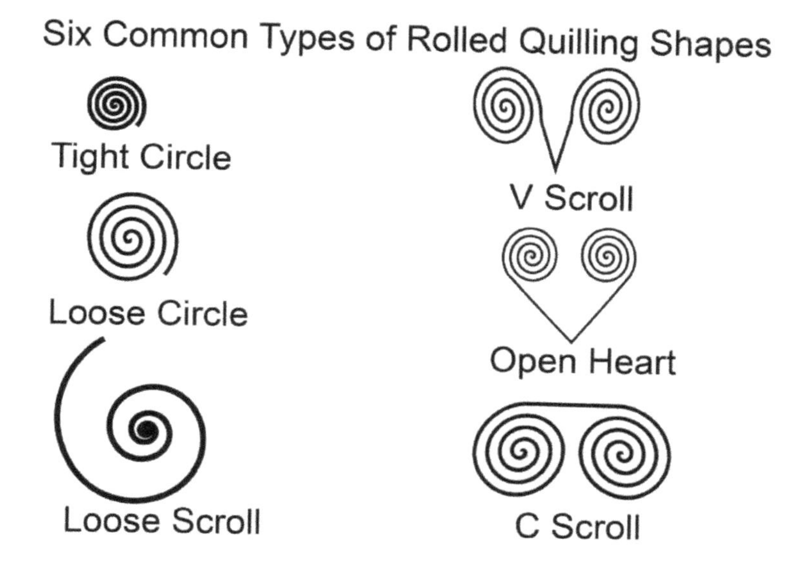

Step 4. Outline Your Letter With Paper Strips

Use your preferred method to apply glue to the pieces of paper that will form the frame of your letter.

Note: Glue: Less is More

Too much glue can ruin your project, so be careful. There are two ways to apply glue to your straight strips of paper that form the frame of your letter. (Use either of these methods to place your shaped and quilled pieces inside the letter frame, too.)

- Use a small brush and a light touch to apply glue to the edge of the paper.
- Place the strips lightly onto a paper plate with glue to lightly coat the edge of a piece, then place on your outline.

Step 5. Frame the Outside of the Letter With Paper Strips

- Glue and place your strips on the outline of your letter. Hold each strip down gently until the glue is firm enough for the strip of paper to stand up on its own.
- Make a crisp fold on a strip of paper and add a drop of glue on each end and overlap it on each corner. This small strip will secure the corners.
- Glue and layer a quarter-inch strip as an anchor anywhere else you have a joined strip of paper creating the wall. The layering will make the frame stronger.

- Allow the wall of your quilled letter to dry thoroughly.

Step 6. Begin Filling in Your Letter Frame

Once you have built your outside frame, fill in the insides of your monogram.

- Follow your design and glue your shapes and strips into place, using your fingers and tweezers for tight spaces.
- Allow the finished piece to dry completely for a few hours.

half finished quilled monogram letter R

Step 7. Use Your Tweezers

Tweezers are a quillers best friend. They are one of the most important tools you will use because it helps you pull paper shapes of all sizes into small spaces inside your monogram project without disturbing the frame.

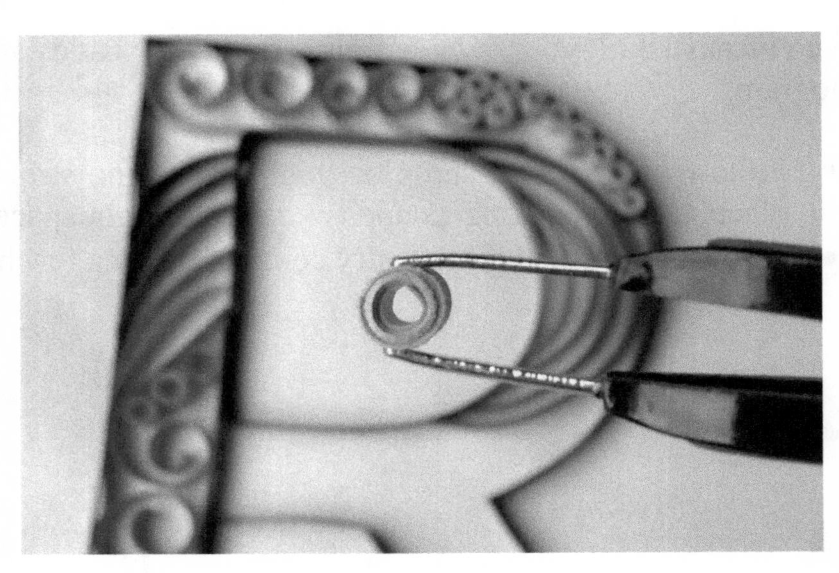

Step 8. Frame the Finished Quilled Monogram

When your piece is dry, place it in your shadowbox frame.

Note: The Importance of a Shadowbox Frame

A standard picture frame with glass is not deep enough to house your quilled monogram. You will need a shadowbox that is at least an inch deep in order to accommodate the raised surface of the quilled project.

Printed in the USA
CPSIA information can be obtained
at www.ICGtesting.com
LVHW041100170624
783379LV00021B/337